Step-by-Step

Mosaics

Michelle Powell

Heinemann
LIBRARY

www.heinemann.co.uk
Visit our website to find out more information about
Heinemann Library books

To order:
 Phone 44 (0) 1865 888066

 Send a fax to 44 (0) 1865 314091

 Visit the Heinemann Bookshop at www.heinemann.co.uk to
browse our catalogue and order online

Produced by Search Press Limited in Great Britain 2001.
First published by Heinemann Library, Halley Court, Jordan Hill, Oxford
OX2 8EJ, a division of Reed Educational and Professional Publishing Ltd.
Heinemann is a registered trademark of Reed Educational & Professional
Publishing Limited.

OXFORD   MELBOURNE   AUCKLAND
JOHANNESBURG   BLANTYRE   GABORONE
IBADAN   PORTSMOUTH NH (USA)   CHICAGO

Text copyright © Michelle Powell 2001
Photographs by Search Press Studios
Photographs and design copyright © Search Press Limited 2001

The moral right of the proprietor has been asserted.

Originated by Graphics '91 Pte Ltd., Singapore
Printed in Hong Kong

ISBN 0 43111 177 4 (paperback)
05 04 03 02 01
10 9 8 7 6 5 4 3 2 1

ISBN 0 43111 167 7 (hardback)
04 03
10 9 8 7 6 5 4 3 2

British Library Cataloguing in Publication Data

Powell, Michelle
Mosaics. – (Step-by-Step)
1.Mosaics – Technique – Juvenile literature
I.Title
738.5

Acknowledgements
The Publishers would like to thank the Bridgeman Art Library for permission to
reproduce the photograph on page 5.

> *This book is dedicated to all my family,
> but mostly to Gemma, Hayley, Rikki,
> Tara, Dan, Lynsey, James and Natalie.*

*With many thanks to all the children involved
in the making of this book, to all the staff and
friends at Search Press and especially to Mum
and Dad for their continuous help and support,
not only through the writing of this book, but
also all the other events along the way.*

• •

*The Publishers would like to say a huge thank
you to Brandon Pitchers, Toby Dowling,
Rheanna Wood, Rochelle Wood, Robert
Sharma, Rebecca Theobald, Hannah Perry and
Nicole Fields.*

*Special thanks are also due to Southborough
Primary School, Tunbridge Wells.*

> (!)
> When this sign is used in the
> book, it means that adult
> supervision is needed.
>
> **REMEMBER!**
> Ask an adult to help you
> when you see this sign.

KM

Contents

Introduction

Traditional mosaics are beautiful works of art. They are created with many small pieces of clay, glass, stone and other hard materials, which are set closely together on a firm surface to create a decorative design or picture.

The earliest mosaics date back to 3000 BC when they were usually created as a type of floor decoration made of small coloured pebbles. Later, glass, marble and clay were coloured then cut into small cubes or tiles. These were used to decorate the floors, walls and ceilings inside important buildings. A thick layer of plaster would be applied to the wall, then a picture or design was painted on to the surface while it was still wet. Before the plaster dried, matching coloured cubes or tiles were pushed into the surface to create the mosaic.

Large mosaics took a long time to make and were expensive, so they were very precious and a sign of great wealth. They were mostly used to decorate the inside of churches and religious buildings. Early Christian mosaics show figures and animals with decorative borders. In Islam, temples were decorated with beautiful designs of leaves and palm trees with a vibrant gold background. The Greeks often decorated their floors with dark and light pebble mosaics.

The ancient Egyptians made mosaic jewellery for their kings by setting tiny pieces of turquoise, precious stones and enamel into gold. On page 16 you will see how you can create a similar type of jewellery using pasta painted gold and turquoise. Gold and turquoise were also used to decorate statues and pottery items made by the ancient craft workers of Latin America. The Greeks and Romans made huge mosaics from handmade coloured clay tiles and our coaster project on page 20 shows you how to make your own clay mosaic tiles.

Some early mosaics can still be seen today, as they have not worn away over time. Now, small coloured glass squares and highly glazed clay tiles are especially made, and although they take a long time to create and are very expensive, mosaics are still being made by skilled crafts people.

__Opposite__ The best-known mosaics were made by Roman and Byzantine craft workers. The mosaic pictured on the right was designed to decorate the church of S. Vitale in Ravenna, Italy, in about 530 AD. It shows soldiers at the court of the Byzantine emperor Justinian. Large mosaics were probably designed by companies of artists, and the pieces, the tessarae, were cut before being taken to a building to be stuck in place.

5

Materials

The items pictured here are the basic tools and equipment you will need to make the projects shown in this book. Mosaics can be created using many different small objects and you will already have some of these at home. Other items will be easy to find in your local shops. In addition, specific items are needed for certain projects, such as shearing elastic, a felt tip pen, a wooden rolling pin, cord, pliers, sequins, coloured metallic trim and feathers. You should check the list of materials carefully before you start each project.

Note Whenever you use paints, glue or clay, you should cover your working area with newspaper. Wear old clothes and work on a tidy, flat surface. Have a damp cloth at the ready in case of spills, and tidy up when you have finished creating your mosaic.

All sorts of things can be decorated with mosaics. **Wood**, **terracotta** and **card** are ideal, but so are **fabric**, **paper** and **biscuits**.

It is possible to mosaic with all sorts of materials. You can use **pebbles**, **high-density foam**, **card** and **felt**, and even **eggshells**, **pasta** and **sweets**. Wonderful mosaic effects can be created with other things too – **air-drying clay**, **foil** and even **chains**, **screws**, **washers**, **nuts** and **bolts**.

Mosaic designs can be secured using **PVA glue**, **a glue stick** or **fabric glue** – be sure to read the manufacturer's instructions carefully. You should use **icing** when sticking sweets to biscuits. Icing is made by mixing icing sugar and lemon juice in a **bowl**.

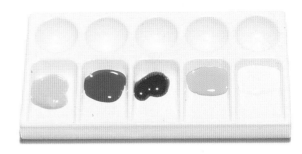

A **palette** is useful for paints, but an old china plate will do just as well. **Water-based paint** is used for the projects in this book. Coloured pens can be used instead of paint if you wish.

A **cocktail stick** is used to measure and adjust the gaps between mosaic pieces.

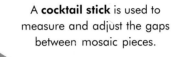

Scissors are used to cut paper, card, foil, fabric, cord and string.

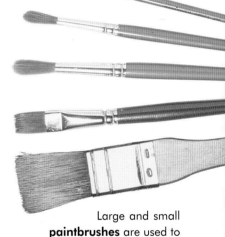

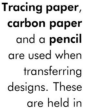

A **hole punch** is used to make neat, round holes.

Large and small **paintbrushes** are used to apply PVA glue and paint.

A **knife** is used for cutting clay and **spoons** for mixing lemon juice and icing sugar.

A **ruler** is used as a guide when drawing straight lines and when trimming clay.

Tracing paper, **carbon paper** and a **pencil** are used when transferring designs. These are held in place with **masking tape**.

Newspaper is used to cover your work surface.

Insect Greetings Card

It is very easy to make attractive mosaic greetings cards for your family and friends using your own drawings or paintings. Make sure you paint or draw them on thick card using brightly coloured, bold designs. Strong images and patterns work best, as fine detail will be lost when the picture is cut into mosaic pieces. Draw a grid on to the front of the picture or photograph (see step 4) and cut along the lines to create your mosaic pieces.

YOU WILL NEED
Thin card
Medium weight card
Carbon paper • Tracing paper
Masking tape • Pencil
Scissors • Ruler
Water-based paints or coloured pens
Paintbrush • Glue stick
Cocktail stick

1 Fold a piece of thin card in half and place it to one side.

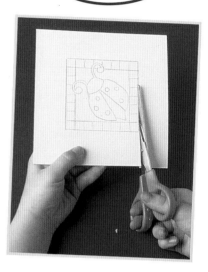

2 Transfer the insect pattern shown on page 29 on to a piece of medium weight card. Cut around the edge.

3 Use coloured paints or pens to fill in the design.

4 Use a pencil and ruler to join up the lines on the border – to form a grid on the front of the design.

8

5

Cut along each line using scissors. Carefully lay the pieces down in order as they are cut out.

6

Carefully glue the pieces in the right order on to the front of the folded card. Leave a 2mm ($^1/_{12}$in) gap between each piece, using a cocktail stick as a guide.

FURTHER IDEAS

Use a colour photocopy of a favourite photograph instead of drawing your own picture.

African Mask

Masks were worn in African tribal war dances to make the wearer look more ferocious. The dancers would also use body adornments and sometimes special clothing, which added to the drama and atmosphere of the dance. You can make your own African mosaic mask using small squares and triangles of thin coloured high-density foam, felt or thin card. These soft materials are excellent for masks as they are more comfortable than some of the harder materials that are available.

YOU WILL NEED

Coloured high-density foam
Carbon paper • Tracing paper
Masking tape • Pencil
Scissors • Felt tipped pen
PVA glue • Hole punch
Shearing elastic

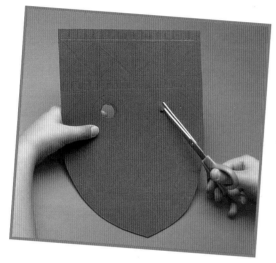

1 Transfer the mask pattern shown on page 29 on to a piece of high-density foam. Cut around the basic shape. Hold the mask up to your face, then carefully feel around on the front for the position of your eyes. Ask a friend to mark in their position with a felt-tipped pen, then cut out the eye holes using scissors.

2 Use the pattern as a rough guide. Choosing different colours, cut squares, triangles and wedge shapes from high-density foam.

3 Glue the pieces on to the mask using PVA glue.

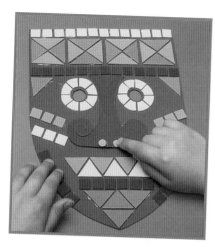

Cut out the nose from another piece of high-density foam and glue it into position. Cut out two circles for the nostrils and glue them on to the nose. Leave the glue to dry for half an hour.

Use a hole punch to make a hole on either side of the mask, approximately 1cm (½in) in from the edge.

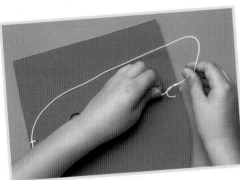

6
Cut a piece of shearing elastic so that it is long enough to fit around your head. Tie each end through the holes in the mask.

FURTHER IDEAS

Choose an animal and make a fun mask, or choose different colours and create your own African mask.

Knight in Armour Picture

In the Middle Ages battling knights wore armour made of metal sheets and chain mail, which protected them from injury. In order to make this knight look more realistic, metal nuts, bolts, screws, washers and chain have been used, along with coloured and silver foils. You do not have to use any of these – just create the knight with whatever you have. Real chain has been used to create the chain mail. You can buy this from most DIY and home improvement stores.

YOU WILL NEED

Thick coloured card
Silver and coloured foil
Selection of small nuts, bolts, washers, screws and chain
Carbon paper • Tracing paper
Masking tape • Pencil • Scissors
Water-based paint • Pliers
Small paintbrush
PVA glue

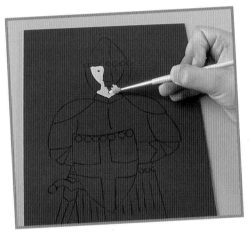

1

Transfer the knight in armour and shield patterns shown on page 29 on to a piece of thick card. Paint in the knight's face using a small paintbrush.

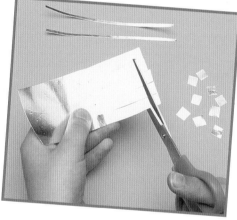

2

Cut silver foil into small squares, triangles and wedge shapes for the armour. Cut out two strips long enough for the sword.

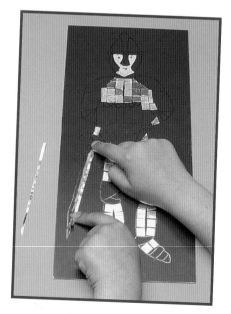

3

Glue the foil on to the knight using PVA glue.

4

Roll pieces of silver foil into small balls. Use PVA glue to attach them to the cuff on the armour, and the helmet.

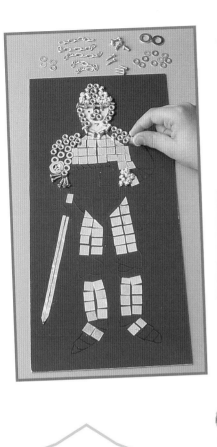

5

Position the nuts, bolts, washers, screws and chain carefully on the knight. Glue in place with PVA glue.

If you decide to include chain, ask an adult to pull it apart with pliers, to make the correct lengths.

6

Cut out squares of coloured foil. Decorate the shield with the squares and washers then glue them into position with PVA glue. Leave to dry overnight.

FURTHER IDEAS

Make a metal robot picture using the same techniques, or create a shiny alien.

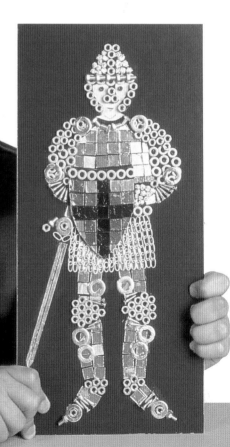

Indian Elephant Shoebag

In India, elephants are often seen at festivals wearing bright, colourful decorative saddlecloths and elaborate headdresses. Using coloured felt or fabrics, feathers and pretty gold or metallic coloured trims, you can create a fabric Indian elephant mosaic on a plain shoe or toiletries bag. If you do not have one that is suitable, ask an adult to make a simple bag out of a rectangle of fabric. Fold this in half, sew the bottom edges together, then the side edges. Turn the top edge over to the inside to form a hem, then sew along the bottom edge, leaving a gap at the side seam. Thread the cord through the hem and tie a knot at the end.

YOU WILL NEED

Fabric shoebag
Grey and coloured felt
Carbon paper • Tracing paper
Masking tape • Pencil
2 small feathers • Sequins
Metallic coloured trim
Scissors • PVA glue

Cut grey felt into small squares and wedge shapes.

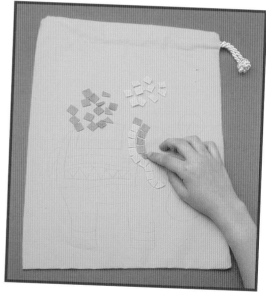

2 Transfer the elephant design shown on page 30 on to your shoebag. Stick the grey felt squares and wedge shapes on to the elephant using PVA glue.

3 Use different colours and cut some more felt into small squares and wedge shapes. Glue them in position.

 4

Use PVA glue to attach small feathers to the headdress, and use sequins to decorate the saddlecloth.

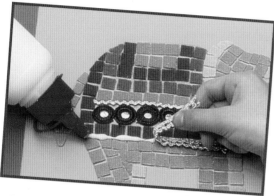

5 Glue metallic coloured trim around the headdress and the base of the saddlecloth.

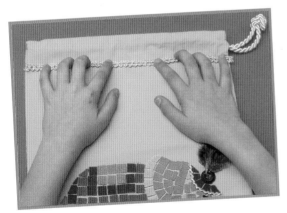

6 Glue metallic coloured trim around the top of the bag to decorate it. Leave to dry overnight.

Note The design on this shoebag is only glued on and therefore the bag should not be washed. If it gets dirty, carefully sponge it clean.

FURTHER IDEAS
Decorate a pencil case, school bag, baseball hat, T-shirt or jacket. Change the colours for different effects.

Egyptian Eagle Necklace

Beautiful gold and precious stone jewellery has been found in the tombs of ancient Egyptian pharaohs. You can make your own dazzling Egyptian mosaic jewellery using dried pasta – all sorts of different shapes are available. Look out for small shells and tubes that can be threaded like beads on to shearing elastic. The pasta is painted using coloured and metallic water-based paints in the same colours as the gold and precious stones used in Egyptian jewellery.

YOU WILL NEED

Small pasta shells and tubes
Thick card • Carbon paper
Tracing paper • Masking tape • Pencil
Metallic and coloured water-based paint
Paintbrush • Newspaper
3 lengths of shearing elastic 80cm
(31½in) long
Scissors • PVA glue
Hole punch

1 Transfer the eagle pattern shown on page 30 on to thick card. Carefully cut it out.

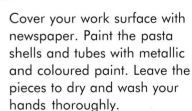

2 Cover your work surface with newspaper. Paint the pasta shells and tubes with metallic and coloured paint. Leave the pieces to dry and wash your hands thoroughly.

Note Do not cook or eat the pasta after it has been painted.

3 Use a hole punch to make three holes at the edge of the eagle's wings.

5

Tie three lengths of shearing elastic through the holes on one side of one wing. Thread pasta tubes on to the elastic.

Note String can be used instead of elastic.

4 Glue the pasta shells and tubes in place using PVA glue.

6 Thread the other end of each piece of shearing elastic through the remaining three holes and tie securely. Glue on more shells to cover the holes.

FURTHER IDEAS

Create a scarab beetle bracelet to match your necklace using the same techniques. Or look for other Egyptian designs and make your own jewellery using different colours.

Maths Biscuits

Mosaics can even be created using edible items like the small coloured sweets in this project. Here, candy coated chocolate sweets are attached to plain biscuits using icing. The quantities given make enough icing for four large biscuits. If you want to decorate more, you will need to make more icing. Use everyday kitchen utensils to make the icing and not things that you would normally use for painting, and remember to wash your hands well before you start to decorate the biscuits.

1 Place six heaped dessertspoons of icing sugar into a bowl.

2 Add four teaspoons of lemon juice.

3 Stir the icing and lemon juice together until all the lumps are gone.

Note The icing should be like a stiff paste. If it is too runny, add more icing sugar. If it is too dry, add a drop more lemon juice.

4 Spoon a small quantity of icing over a biscuit and use the back of a teaspoon to spread it out.

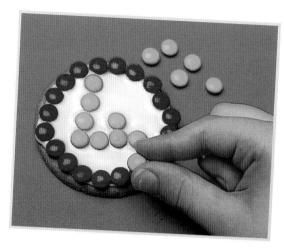

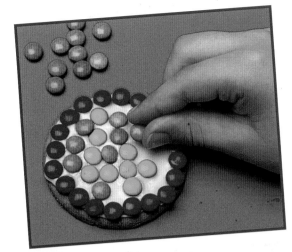

5 Press coloured sweets into the wet icing around the edge of the biscuit. Use a different colour to create a number in the middle.

6 Fill in the spaces around the number with another colour. Leave the biscuit until the icing is set.

FURTHER IDEAS

Why not mosaic your name on top of your birthday cake, or decorate some biscuits with simple shapes.

Grecian Coaster

The Greeks and Romans used small clay tiles to make their mosaics. In this project mosaic tiles are made using air-drying clay. The rolled out clay is soft enough to cut with a knife and most of the pieces are either squares or triangles, so the design can only have straight edges. When the clay is dry, it is painted with traditional Greek colours and the coaster is then sealed with PVA glue to protect it.

YOU WILL NEED
Air-drying clay • Thick card
Newspaper • Knife
Wooden rolling pin • Ruler
Water-based paint
Large and small paintbrushes
Scissors • PVA glue

1 Cover your work surface with newspaper. Take a ball of clay, roughly the size of a tennis ball, and roll it out to a thickness of between 0.5cm and 0.8cm (¼in and ⅜in).

2 Trim off the edges of the clay with a knife, using a ruler as a guide. Cut vertical lines approximately 1cm (½in) apart. Cut horizontal lines in the same way to form small clay squares.

3 Cut a few of the squares diagonally to make triangles. Leave the clay to dry for two days.

Knives can be sharp. Ask an adult to help you cut the clay.

Use a small paintbrush and different colours to paint the squares and triangles.

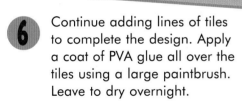

5 Cut out a piece of thick card roughly 11cm (4¼in) square. Using the design shown on page 30 as a guide, start to build up the mosaic design. Secure the tiles with PVA glue and work line by line.

6 Continue adding lines of tiles to complete the design. Apply a coat of PVA glue all over the tiles using a large paintbrush. Leave to dry overnight.

Note When PVA glue is dry, it can be very difficult to remove, so wear an apron or old shirt to protect your clothes.

FURTHER IDEAS
You can make matching place mats and pot stands using this technique.

Seaside Pebble Frame

Small pebbles are great for making mosaics. You can sometimes find coloured ones on the beach, but you could paint the pebbles yourself if you could not find any. I have used white pebbles about the size of a pea and very small pebbles that have been painted after they have been glued down. Pearlescent paint has been used for a shimmering effect, which makes the picture frame look more colourful, but you can use any colour. Choose a frame with a very wide and flat border to give you plenty of space for your design, and use it to display your own drawing, painting or photograph.

YOU WILL NEED
Plain wooden frame
Selection of small pebbles
Newspaper • Carbon paper
Tracing paper • Masking tape
Pencil • Water-based paint
Paintbrush
PVA glue

 Transfer the patterns shown on page 31 on to your frame. Draw some waves in the background and then paint them, working from the top to the bottom.

 Apply PVA glue around the edge of the starfish, over the fish's body and around the edge of the fish's tail.

3 Sprinkle very small pebbles over the wet glue to decorate the starfish and fish. Leave to dry for at least fifteen minutes.

4 Tip the frame over a piece of newspaper to remove excess pebbles. These can be saved and used for another project.

5 Paint the small pebbles on the fish and the starfish in colours of your choice.

6 Apply glue to the centre of the starfish. Add stripes of glue to the fish's body and tail, and lines of glue following the shape of the waves. Press larger pebbles into the glue, then leave to dry overnight.

FURTHER IDEAS

Cover the top of a box, or make decorative pebble pictures using this technique.

Celestial Pot

All sorts of materials can be used to create a mosaic. Here broken eggshells are glued on to a plain terracotta plant pot. The theme is the sky above – one side shows a sun, the other a moon and star. For a small pot like this you will need the shells of three eggs. If your pot is larger, you will need more. Use the completed pot for an indoor plant, as the mosaic will not be weatherproof.

YOU WILL NEED

Terracotta pot
Eggshells • Newspaper
Carbon paper • Tracing paper
Masking tape • Pencil
Water-based metallic paint
Paintbrush • PVA glue
Cocktail stick

1 Wash the eggshells in warm water then place them on newspaper. Leave to dry.

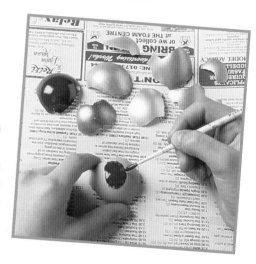

2 Break the eggshells carefully into large pieces, then paint them with different colours. Leave to dry.

3 Transfer the patterns shown on page 31 on to your pot. Apply PVA glue to one of the areas of the design.

4 Break the eggshells into smaller pieces. Firmly press one of the pieces on to the wet glue to break the shell up further.

5 Use a cocktail stick to push the pieces of eggshell apart, leaving small gaps in between.

6 Continue applying different colours to your design. Finish by filling in around the design with more eggshells and leave to dry.

FURTHER IDEAS

Create a beautiful jewellery box by decorating a plain wooden box with brightly coloured eggshells.

Aztec Book Cover

This book cover is inspired by the wonderful colours of the Aztecs. You can transform a cheap, plain, bound notebook easily with the bold geometric pattern. Detailed mosaic designs can take many hours to complete, but here the design is very quick, as the mosaic is created on a printing block that is then used to print a pattern over and over again. You can use many colours on this block and print instant designs.

YOU WILL NEED

Plain book
High-density foam
Thick card • Scissors
Water-based paint
Paintbrush • PVA glue
Cord • Bead

1 Cut high-density foam into small squares and triangles, using the design on page 31 as a rough guide.

2 Cut out a square of thick card, roughly the size of the design. Glue the foam pieces on to the card using PVA glue, following the lines of the design, to create a printing block. Leave to dry.

3 Apply a thin layer of paint to the foam squares and triangles using a small paintbrush and colours of your choice.

4 Press the printing block on to the front of your book.

5 Repeat, applying more paint each time. Complete a stripe down one side of the book. Leave to dry.

6 Loop a length of cord around the book, then thread a tightly-fitting bead through to secure it.

FURTHER IDEAS

Create your own mosaic design using different shapes, then stamp the design on to a picture frame.

Patterns

You can trace the patterns on these pages straight from the book (step 1). Alternatively, you can make them larger or smaller on a photocopier if you wish, and then follow steps 2–4.

Ask an adult to help you enlarge the patterns on a photocopier.

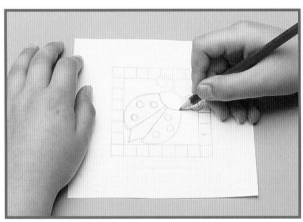

1 Place a piece of tracing paper over the pattern, then tape it down with small pieces of masking tape. Trace around the outline using a soft pencil.

2 Place carbon paper face down on the surface you want to transfer the design on to. Place the tracing or photocopy over the top and tape it in place.

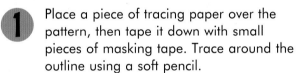

3 Trace over the outline with a pencil.

4 Remove the tracing paper and carbon paper to reveal the transferred image.

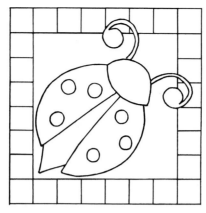

Patterns for the Insect Greetings Cards
featured on pages 8–9.

Patterns for the Knight in Armour
Picture featured on pages 12–13.

Pattern for the African Mask
featured on pages 10–11.

Pattern for the Indian Elephant Shoebag featured on pages 14–15.

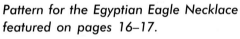

Pattern for the Egyptian Eagle Necklace featured on pages 16–17.

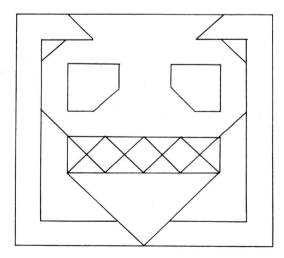

Pattern for the Grecian Coaster featured on pages 20–21.

Patterns for the Celestial Pot featured on pages 24–25.

Patterns for the Seaside Pebble Frame featured on pages 22–23.

Pattern for the Aztec Book Cover featured on pages 26–27.

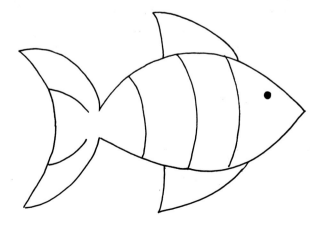

Index